Earth's Environment in Danger

Deforestation and Habitat Loss

W9-CNC-938

Jaime Simmons

PowerKiDS press.

New York

Published in 2018 by The Rosen Publishing Group, Inc.
29 East 21st Street, New York, NY 10010

First Edition

Editor: Elizabeth Krajnik
Book Design: Rachel Rising

Photo Credits: Cover Marcelo Horn/E+/Getty Images; Cover, pp. 1, 3, 4, 6, 8, 10, 12, 13, 14, 16, 18, 20, 22, 23, 24 (background) ALKRO/Shutterstock.com; p. 5 Courtesy of NASA Image and Video Library; p. 6 nije salam/Shutterstock.com; p. 7 jodrum/Shutterstock.com; p. 8 Tatjana Kabanova/Shutterstock.com; p. 9 Gideon Ikigai/Shutterstock.com; p. 11 Kletr/Shutterstock.com; p. 12 aaabbbccc/ Shutterstock.com; p. 13 Byelikova Oksana/Shutterstock.com; p. 15 Artush/ Shutterstock.com; p. 16 Jay Ondreicka/Shutterstock.com; p. 17 Soundaholic studio/ Shutterstock.com; p. 19 (top) LanaElcova/Shutterstock.com; p. 19 (bottom) Michal Sanca/Shutterstock.com; p. 21 Brazil Photos/LightRocket/Getty Images; p. 22 ProStockStudio/Shutterstock.com.

Library of Congress Cataloging-in-Publication Data

Names: Simmons, Jaime, author.
Title: Deforestation and habitat loss / Jaime Simmons.
Description: New York : PowerKids Press, [2018] | Series: Earth's environment in danger | Includes index.
Identifiers: LCCN 2017031897| ISBN 9781538325353 (library bound) | ISBN 9781538326053 (pbk.) | ISBN 9781538326060 (6 pack)
Subjects: LCSH: Deforestation–Juvenile literature. | Forest ecology–Juvenile literature. | Nature–Effect of human beings on–Juvenile literature. | Conservation of natural resources–Juvenile literature.
Classification: LCC SD418 .S56 2018 | DDC 333.75/13–dc23
LC record available at https://lccn.loc.gov/2017031897

Manufactured in the United States of America

CPSIA Compliance Information: Batch #BW18PK: For Further Information contact Rosen Publishing, New York, New York at 1-800-237-9932

Contents

What Is Deforestation? 4

Types of Deforestation 6

Forest Homes 8

Earth's Lungs 10

Case Study: Madagascar 12

Types of Habitat Loss 16

Causes of Habitat Loss in
     the United States 18

Reducing the Effects 20

What Can You Do? 22

Glossary 23

Index. 24

Websites. 24

What Is Deforestation?

Deforestation is when forests are destroyed so the land can be used for other purposes. Each year, about 18 million acres (7.3 million ha) of forests are destroyed. Forests are very important for life on Earth. Without forests, many species, or kinds, of plants and animals will lose their habitats, or natural homes.

Even though deforestation happens all over the world, rain forests are some of the areas in which deforestation happens the most. This is because rain forests are home to important **resources**, including wood, soil rich in **nutrients** for farming, and **minerals**.

[Danger Alert!]

In Bolivia, about 865,000 acres (350,053 ha) of land are deforested each year. That's nearly the size of Rhode Island!

These aerial images of the Amazon rain forest in Brazil show just how much green space has been lost to deforestation.

Mato Grosso, Brazil, 1992

Mato Grosso, Brazil, 2006

Types of Deforestation

Deforestation can be a natural process. Fires claim large parts of forests throughout the world each year. However, many of these fires start because of human activities. Most deforestation is linked to humans in one way or another.

One of the biggest causes of deforestation is **agriculture**. Farmers destroy a patch of forest to grow crops or raise their livestock. Some farmers create this space by cutting down the trees and burning them. This process is called slash-and-burn agriculture.

Logging is another cause of deforestation. Logging provides raw **material**—wood—for the paper and lumber **industries**.

Slash-and-burn agriculture creates ash, which contains nutrients that are good for farming. It also prevents weeds from growing. However, after a few years of crop growing, the soil is no longer as healthy and the weeds return.

Forest Homes

Forests are important for a number of reasons. Perhaps the most important reason is that they're home to many different species of plants and animals.

About 80 percent of the plants and animals on Earth live in forests. Humans live in and depend on forests, too. About 300 million people live in forests and 1.6 billion people depend on them to make a living.

Can you imagine walking home from school one day and finding your house burned down or simply gone? This is what it's like for many animals living in places experiencing deforestation.

squirrel monkeys

How many plant and animal species do you think live in just this small part of the forest? Trees provide shelter for our forest friends.

9

Earth's Lungs

Trees and other plants are necessary for maintaining life on Earth. Forests act as Earth's lungs. Plants take in a gas called carbon dioxide. Through **photosynthesis**, they break down carbon dioxide and release oxygen. Most life on Earth depends on oxygen to survive.

During photosynthesis, trees and other plants don't use up all of the carbon from the carbon dioxide. They keep a portion of the carbon and store it in their **biomass**. When humans cut down and burn trees and other plants, this carbon is released into the **atmosphere**. This extra carbon dioxide in the air is dangerous to life on Earth.

[Danger Alert!]

About half the world's carbon is stored in the "thick forests" of the Americas' tropical rain forests. Plants in other forests and the world's savannas also store much carbon. Forests and savannas must be protected from deforestation.

Carbon **emissions** from burning coal to produce electricity create **greenhouse gases**. In 2015, power plants accounted for 29 percent of the total greenhouse gas emissions in the United States.

Case Study: Madagascar

Madagascar is home to many different plant and animal species. The island split from Africa about 150 million years ago. Its plants and animals changed over time to survive there. Many of these plants and animals are endemic species, which means they don't exist anywhere else on Earth.

Plants in Madagascar are evergreen, which means they can photosynthesize year round. This is just one of many general adaptations, or changes, the plants have to survive in their environment.

Deforestation started out on a small scale after the island became a French colony in 1896. Due to greater deforestation that has been taking place since the 1940s, Madagascar now has less than 10 percent of its original forest cover.

Much of this deforestation was a result of human activities such as cutting down trees for precious wood and building railroads.

[Danger Alert!]

All of the world's lemurs are native to the island of Madagascar and most of them are in danger of dying out. Today, many species of plants and animals native to Madagascar are at risk of going extinct, or dying out completely, due to deforestation.

lemurs

About 1940, **vaccines** were introduced in Madagascar. Before this, many people died from a number of diseases. Because fewer people were dying from disease, the population began to increase. As a result, forests in Madagascar were cleared to provide resources for the people. Madagascar's population continues to increase and is expected to reach 28 million by 2025.

Before 1950, farmers cleared patches of forest on a small scale. Starting about that time, deforestation increased as a way to pay off the money the country owed. The forests were cleared, the wood was sold to other countries, and cash crops were planted to make money for the island's inhabitants.

[Danger Alert!]

When Madagascar became a French colony, its forests covered about 27.7 million acres (11.2 million ha). By 1950, these forests were reduced to about 18.8 million acres (7.6 million ha). Between 1950 and 1985, these forests were further reduced to about 9.4 million acres (3.8 million ha).

Growing coffee—Madagascar's most important trade crop—has led to soil erosion, which means the soil is worn away, in part during storms in the rainy season.

Types of Habitat Loss

Earth's habitats are key to the survival of plant and animal life.

Habitat destruction refers to when a habitat becomes unable to support the kinds of life that once lived there. Deforestation is an example of habitat destruction.

Habitat degradation occurs when natural forces or human activities affect habitats over time. This causes the habitat to be unable to support life as well as it did in the past.

Habitat fragmentation means that habitats are divided into different areas. This can happen as a result of human activities, such as building dams, or natural processes, such as earthquakes.

Pollution can lead to habitat degradation and habitat fragmentation. This picture shows a water habitat affected by pollution. As a result, some of the fish there have died.

Causes of Habitat Loss in the United States

Habitat loss happens all over the world, not just in forests. In the United States, natural processes and human activities affect many different habitats. Some scientists believe that about 46 percent of the United States was covered in forest before the Europeans arrived.

As humans have become more advanced, the way in which we interact with the earth has changed. Humans have cut down large patches of forest for agriculture and for space to build roads, offices, shopping malls, and housing developments. Dams and pollution affect our water sources and can lead to water shortages.

[Danger Alert!]

Global warming has led to serious habitat loss. As sea levels and temperatures rise, animals risk losing their homes, becoming endangered, or even dying out completely.

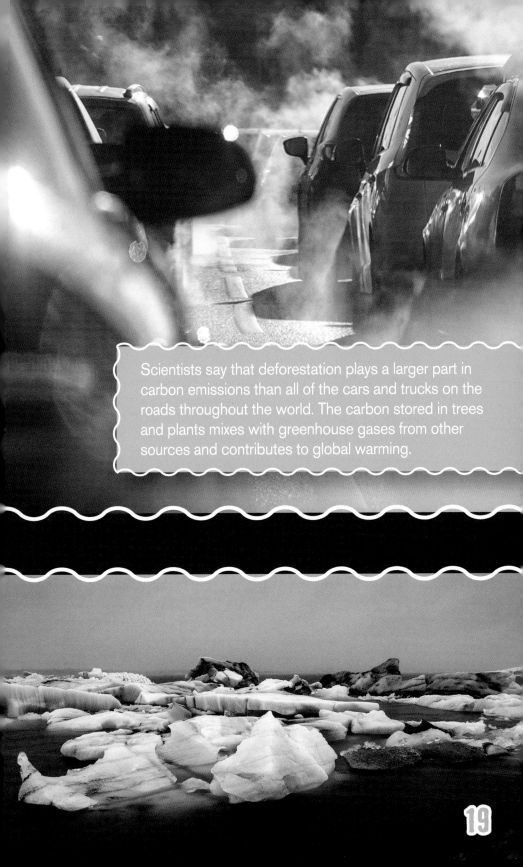

Scientists say that deforestation plays a larger part in carbon emissions than all of the cars and trucks on the roads throughout the world. The carbon stored in trees and plants mixes with greenhouse gases from other sources and contributes to global warming.

Reducing the Effects

A number of countries throughout the world have recognized that deforestation is adding to the world's **environmental** issues. Some of these countries are trying to lessen the effects of deforestation by participating in the United Nations' Reducing Emissions from Deforestation and Forest Degradation (REDD+) program.

The REDD+ program places value on the carbon stored in forests and provides money to countries with rain forests to give people reasons to stop deforestation. The lower the rate of deforestation, the more money the country receives from the program. This helps those who own the land continue to make money while keeping the land healthy.

[Danger Alert!]

Clear-cutting, which is when an entire forest is cut down, is one of the worst forms of deforestation. However, if we can stop this practice, we may be able to keep a number of plant and animal species from going extinct.

Since 2008, Brazil has slowed its rate of deforestation by 40 percent. It may reduce deforestation by 80 percent by 2020. This was made possible by the REDD+ program.

21

What Can You Do?

Stopping or even decreasing deforestation is one of the most effective ways to lessen carbon emissions that contribute to global warming. You can help stop deforestation and save the forest habitats of the world.

When you go to the store, encourage your family to purchase locally grown foods and recyclable packaging. This will help reduce the need to continue deforestation.

Speaking up for what you believe in is also a good way to help save our forests. Calling your local members of Congress can help keep government agencies like the Environmental Protection Agency working toward a better future.

agriculture: The practice of growing crops and raising livestock.

atmosphere: The whole mass of air that surrounds Earth.

biomass: Plant matter and animal waste used as a source of fuel.

emission: Something that is given off.

environmental: Having to do with the natural world.

greenhouse gas: Gases in the atmosphere that trap energy from the sun.

industry: A group of businesses that provide a certain product or service.

material: Something from which something else can be made.

mineral: A matter that is naturally formed under the ground.

nutrient: Something taken in by a plant or animal that helps it grow and stay healthy.

photosynthesis: The way in which green plants make their own food from sunlight, water, and carbon dioxide.

resource: Something that can be used.

vaccine: A matter given to a person or an animal to help protect them from a particular disease.

Index

A
Africa, 12
agriculture, 6, 7, 18
animals, 4, 8, 9, 12, 13, 16, 18, 20
atmosphere, 10

B
biomass, 10
Bolivia, 4
Brazil, 5, 21

C
carbon dioxide, 10
carbon emissions, 11, 19, 22
coffee, 15

E
endemic species, 12
Environmental Protection Agency, 22
erosion, 15

G
global warming, 18, 19, 22
greenhouse gases, 11, 19

H
habitat degradation, 16, 17
habitat destruction, 16
habitat fragmentation, 16, 17

L
lemurs, 13
logging, 6

M
Madagascar, 12, 13, 14, 15
Mato Grosso, 5

O
oxygen, 10

P
photosynthesis, 10, 12
plants, 4, 8, 9, 10, 12, 13, 16, 19, 20
pollution, 17, 18

R
rain forests, 4, 5, 10, 20
REDD+ program, 20, 21

S
savanna, 10
slash-and-burn agriculture, 6, 7

U
United Nations, 20
United States, 11, 18

Websites

Due to the changing nature of Internet links, PowerKids Press has developed an online list of websites related to the subject of this book. This site is updated regularly. Please use this link to access the list:
www.powerkidslinks.com/eeid/habitat